THE DIGITAL WORLD

LEARN THE LANGUAGE OF

DIGITAL TECH

BY WILLIAM ANTHONY

Enslow
PUBLISHING

Published in 2022 by Enslow Publishing, LLC
101 W. 23rd Street, Suite 240
New York, NY 10011

Cataloging-in-Publication Data

Names: Anthony, William.
Title: Learn the language of digital tech / William
Anthony.
Description: New York : Enslow Publishing, 2022. |
Series: The digital world
Identifiers: ISBN 9781978524798 (pbk.) | ISBN
9781978524811 (library bound) | ISBN 9781978524804
(6 pack) | ISBN 9781978524828 (ebook)
Subjects: LCSH: Information technology--Juvenile
literature. | Digital communications--Juvenile literature.
Classification: LCC T58.5 W555 2022 | DDC 004--dc23

Designer: Dan Scase
Editor: Madeline Tyler

Printed in the United States of America
CPSIA compliance information: Batch #BSENS22: For further information contact
Enslow Publishing, New York, New York at 1-800-398-2504

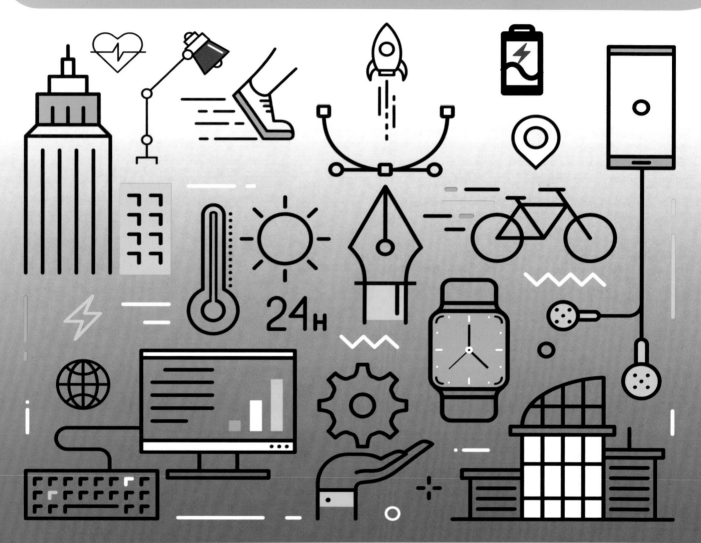

PHOTO CREDITS

HOW TO UNDERSTAND THE LANGUAGE OF DIGITAL TECHNOLOGY

There are lots of strange and interesting pieces of digital technology and just as many words to go with them. This handy guide will help you learn them all. But first, let's take a look at how to understand each word.

ROUTER
(ROU-TUHR)

Noun: a piece of hardware that directs wireless signals, such as an internet connection, to other electronic devices. See **WI-FI**.

HEADWORD: this shows you how a word is spelled. These words are organized in alphabetical order.

PRONUNCIATION GUIDE:

this tells you how to say a word out loud. Say each part exactly how it's written to pronounce the word correctly.

Word class: this is the type of word that the headword is. In this book you will see some of these:
- Noun – a person, place, or thing
- Verb – an action word
- Adjective – a describing word

Abbreviations: this is the type of word that the headword is. In this book you will see some of these:
- Initialism – a set of letters taken from several words that are read as individual letters
- Acronym – a set of letters taken from several words that make a new word

Definition: this is what the headword means.

RELATED WORDS: this shows you other words that link to the one you're looking at.

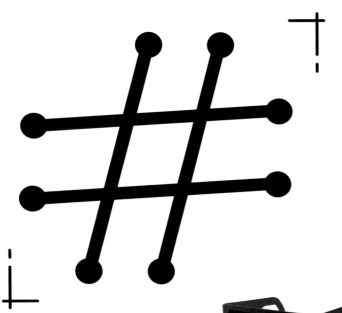

8K

Adjective: used to describe technology or content that provides an extremely sharp on-screen image. It is around eight times the quality of an HD image.

3D ENTERTAINMENT

Noun: images or videos that can be viewed with 3D glasses to give the impression that parts of the image are popping out of the screen towards you.

3D PRINTER

Noun: a machine that allows the user to create a physical object from a computer program. This is normally done by building lots of layers of material on top of each other.

4K

Adjective: used to describe technology or content that provides a very sharp on-screen image. It is around four times the quality of an HD image.

ACCESSIBILITY
(AK-SESS-IH-BIL-IH-TEE)

Adjective: how well and to what degree a device can be used, no matter what the user's abilities or disabilities are. For example, technology can be used to make computers more accessible for people with physical disabilities.

AI (Artificial Intelligence)

Initialism: machines with the ability to carry out tasks that normally require humans. See **ROBOT**.

AIRPLANE MODE

Noun: a setting on phones and other mobile devices that stops calls, texts, and mobile data from being received. Most aircraft will ask you to turn this on while you are flying.

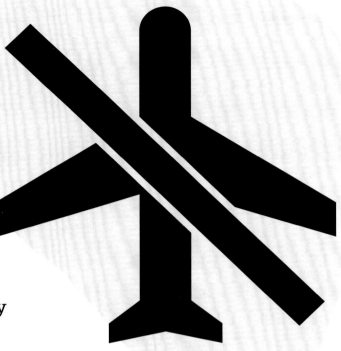

ALWAYS ON DISPLAY

Noun: a feature on some devices that keeps the screen on to display simple information, such as the time, so that the user doesn't have to unlock their phone.

ANDROID
(AN-DROYD)

Noun: an operating system used for smartphones and other devices. Each version of Android is named after a type of food. See **VERSION**.

APP

Noun: short for application. An app is a program installed and used on a computer system or portable device. Types of apps include games, internet browsers, and social media sites.

AR (Augmented Reality)

Initialism: technology that overlays a computer-generated image on top of the user's view of the world, or over a camera's view of the world. See **CGI**.

AUTOMATED
(AW-TOW-MAY-TIHD)

Adjective: operated automatically by a machine, rather than needing a human.

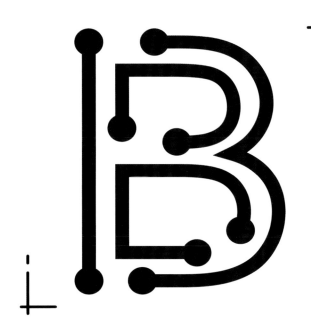

BACKGROUND

Noun: an image that is used behind icons and widgets on your device's home screen. See **WIDGET**.

BATTERY

Noun: a container that stores energy to power a device. Batteries inside mobile devices need to be recharged when they hit 0% or before then.

BATTERY-SAVING MODE

Noun: a feature on many modern devices that limits the device's power in order to save battery life. This mode is useful if you have a very low percentage of battery left and need it to last just a little bit longer.

BLU-RAY

Noun: a type of disc that can hold up to ten times more information than a standard DVD and is usually used to store HD videos. See **DVD** and **HD**.

BRICK

Noun: a slang name given to a type of very old mobile phone that resembled a brick's shape. It is also used to describe how tough and strong this type of phone was.

BUG

Noun: an error in a piece of software that stops it from working the way that it should. See **SOFTWARE**.

CGI (Computer-Generated Imagery)

Initialism: special effects used in TV, games, or films made using computers rather than video cameras. Filmmakers use CGI to create scenes that don't exist in real life.

CLOUD

Noun: the large computers, called servers, that you can connect to on the internet and use for storing data.

CONSOLE

Noun: a system dedicated to playing games.

CROWDFUNDING

Verb: raising money online for new and unique products to be made.

COMMUNICATION TECHNOLOGY

Noun: equipment, such as mobile phones and tablets, that we use to communicate with other people.

COMPATIBLE

Adjective: the ability of a device or computer to work with another device or a program.

CUSTOMIZATION

Noun: a way of changing how something looks or works so that it suits the user better.

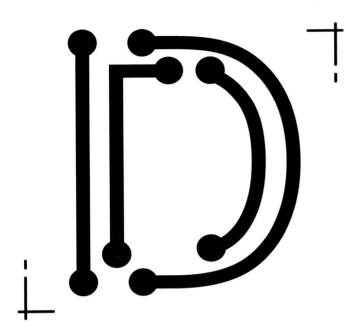

DISPLAY
Noun: the part of an electronic device that shows images to the user.

DRIVERLESS CAR
Noun: a vehicle that uses cameras, lasers, and other technology to drive itself, rather than needing a human to control it.

DIGITAL
Adjective: when something uses and stores information as a series of 1s and 0s to perform specific tasks or functions.

DIGITAL BILLBOARD
Noun: a huge screen that displays digital images that are changed every few seconds by a computer. These are usually used by advertisers.

DID YOU KNOW?

There are different types of self-driving cars. Autonomous cars can drive by themselves using AI but need a human behind the wheel for emergencies. Driverless cars use more complicated AI, and do not need a human or a steering wheel at all. See **AI**.

DIGITAL CAMERA
Noun: a device that is used to take and store photos electronically, rather than on a roll of film.

DRONE

Noun: a flying machine controlled remotely by someone on the ground. Some drones have high-tech cameras that allow the user on the ground to see what the drone sees.

DVD (Digital Versatile Disc)

Initialism: a storage format much like a CD, but with the ability to hold nearly seven times as much information. DVDs are mainly used for video files.

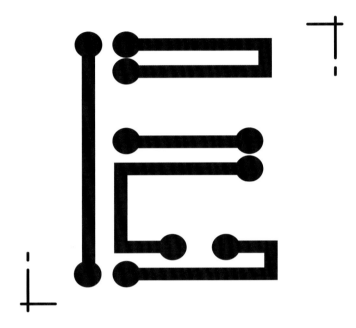

eBOOK

Noun: an electronic version of a book.

EMAIL

Noun: electronic messages that can be sent from one device to another over the internet.

eREADER

Noun: a device on which you can store and read an eBook. See **eBOOK**.

ETHERNET CABLE
(EE-THER-NET CAY-BUHL)

Noun: a wire used to connect devices to each other or to the internet. If your Wi-Fi connection isn't working and you need to access the internet, you might have to use an ethernet cable to connect your computer to your router. See **ROUTER**.

EYE-TRACKING TECHNOLOGY

Noun: technology that allows a device to be controlled using your eye movements. Important uses include helping those who have lost the ability to use their arms to interact with different devices. See **ACCESSIBILITY**.

FACIAL RECOGNITION (FAY-SHUL REH-COG-NIH-SHUN)

Noun: technology that can recognize your face in order to let you unlock your devices or make something work.

FACTORY RESET

Noun: a feature that allows you to return your device to the exact settings it had when it came out of the box. BE CAREFUL! This wipes all of the saved data and information from your device.

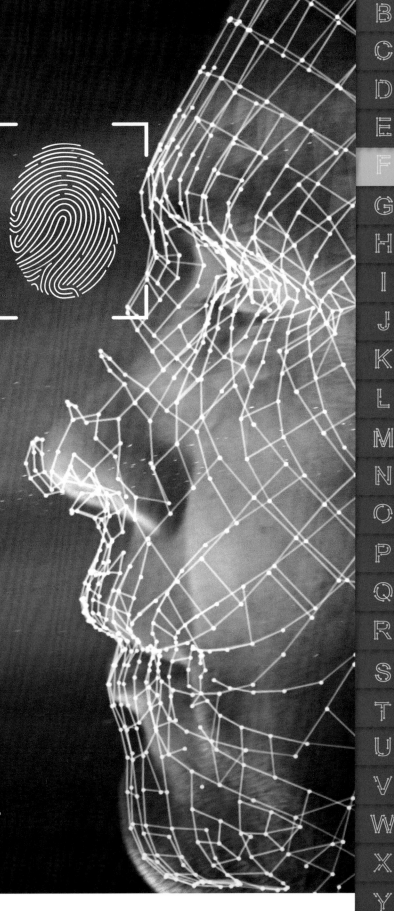

FIBER OPTIC
Adjective: technology that uses light to transmit information.

FINGERPRINT UNLOCK
Noun: a security feature on many devices that allows only the owner of the device to unlock it with their finger.

FITNESS TRACKER
Noun: an electronic device that you can wear that tells you how much exercise you do, your heart rate, and much more.

FLAGSHIP
Noun: the best or most important thing a company has produced.

FLIP PHONE
Noun: a style of phone that bends using a hinge to hide the screen and keys when closed.

FOLDABLE SCREEN
Noun: a display that can be bent in half to make the device smaller or unfolded to increase the size.

HANDS-FREE

Adjective: used to describe something that lets you use a device, such as a smartphone, without using your hands.

HARDWARE

Noun: physical pieces of technology, such as smartphones, keyboards, and touchscreens.

GESTURE CONTROL (JES-CHUR CON-TROL)

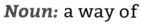

Noun: a way of controlling something using your own movement. For example, some devices might let you wave your hand to the right to skip a song.

HD (High Definition)

Initialism: high-quality graphics that require special screens to view.

HOLOGRAM

Noun: a 3D image created using lights and lasers. Holograms can create the impression that someone is standing in front of you, when the real-life person is actually somewhere else.

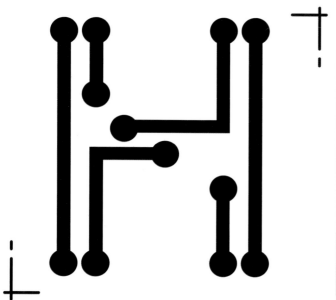

HOTSPOT

Noun: an area in which you can connect to a wireless internet connection.

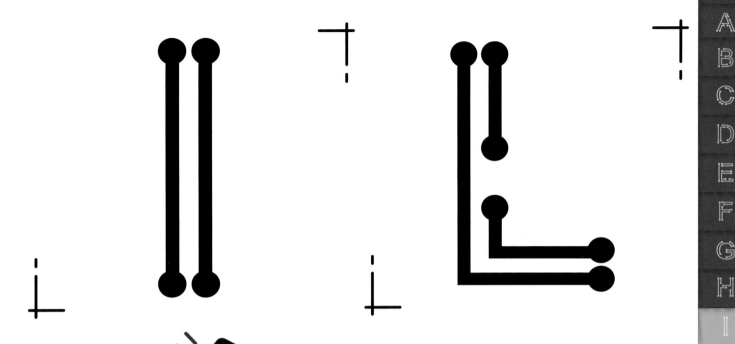

INFRARED

Noun: a type of light that we can't see, which we use in remote controls to control electronics.

INTERNET OF THINGS

Noun: a system where everyday objects, such as a toaster or a fridge, can be connected over the internet.

iOS

Noun: the operating system that Apple uses in its phones and tablets. See **OPERATING SYSTEM**.

iPHONE

Noun: a type of mobile phone that is made by Apple. The first iPhone was released in 2007.

LAPTOP

Noun: a small, foldable personal computer that combines a screen, keyboard, and trackpad in an easy-to-carry format. See **PC**.

LCD (Liquid Crystal Display)

Initialism: a thin and flat electronic screen used in computer monitors and televisions.

LED (Light-Emitting Diode)

Initialism: a small object that creates light when electricity flows through it.

ABCDEFGHIJKLMNOPQRSTUVWXYZ

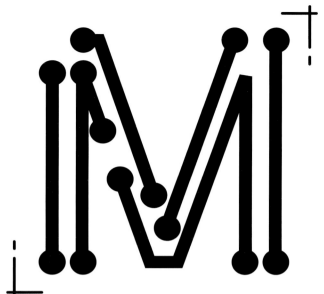

MICROPHONE

Noun: a piece of technology that can turn sound into data, which can be transferred to a speaker or stored as a file.

MANUFACTURER

Noun: a person or company that makes things to be sold.

MEDIA

Noun: ways of communicating information. This could be through writing, photos, videos, or audio, among others.

MEGAPIXEL

Noun: a unit used to measure the quality of a camera or a screen. One megapixel contains around one million pixels. See **PIXELS**.

MOBILE DATA

Noun: internet content that can be accessed by devices such as phones and tablets.

MEMORY CARD

Noun: a small piece of hardware that can be used to store data.

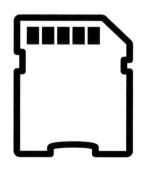

MOBILE PHONE

Noun: a portable telephone with access to radio signals, which allow you to call and interact with people around the world.

MOOD LIGHTING

Noun: bulbs and LEDs that can be set to any color to set the mood or feeling in a room. For example, a deep blue might make a room look very relaxing. See **LED**.

MP3

Noun: a type of audio file that can be downloaded and stored on devices, which allows people to listen to music.

MULTIMEDIA

Noun: combinations of text, graphics, video, animation, and/or sound. See **MEDIA**.

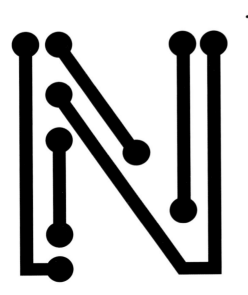

NFC (Near-Field Communication)

Initialism: technology that allows two devices to wirelessly exchange information when they are close to each other.

NOISE-CANCELING HEADPHONES

Noun: a device that you can listen to music through, while blocking out most of the sounds that exist in the world around you.

NOTEBOOK

Noun: a very small and very thin type of laptop. It weighs less than a regular laptop too.

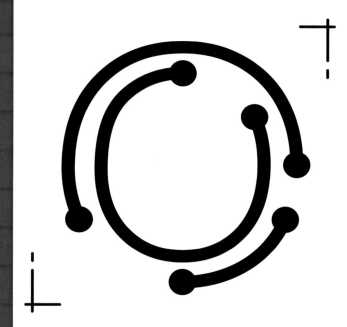

PC (Personal Computer)

Initialism: a piece of hardware that can process and understand bits of data stored as 1s and 0s. See **HARDWARE**.

PERSONAL TRANSPORTER

Noun: a small, two-wheeled vehicle that has a board that can be stood on. The vehicle is controlled by leaning forwards, backwards, to the left, and to the right.

OPERATING SYSTEM

Noun: the main program in a computer that controls the way the device works and makes it possible for other programs to function.

PIN (Personal Identification Number)

Acronym: a short passcode that is used to protect electronic devices or bank cards from being used by anyone other than the owner. Never tell anyone your PIN!

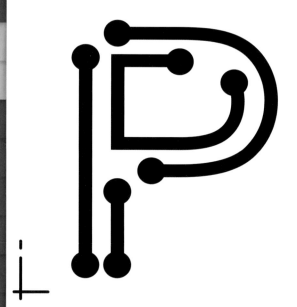

PIXELS

Noun: the tiny units of a digital image. When you look at a picture on a screen, you are looking at a collection of hundreds, thousands, or even hundreds of thousands of tiny colored dots.

PAIRING

Verb: connecting two devices together, usually to transfer information.

POLAROID CAMERA
(POH-LUH-ROYD CAM-RUH)

Noun: a device that takes photos and instantly prints them out rather than storing them on a memory card.

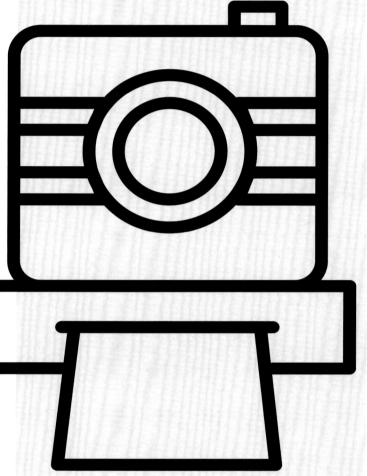

POWER BANK

Noun: a portable device that stores electrical charge, ready to recharge the battery of a smartphone or tablet when you are away from an outlet. See **BATTERY**.

PROJECTOR

Noun: a device used to shine images and videos onto a wall or screen. Projectors are usually used to display images much bigger than TV or computer screens.

PORTRAIT MODE

Noun: a feature in smartphone cameras that creates sharp photos of someone while blurring out the background. See **SMARTPHONE**.

PROTOTYPE

Noun: a trial product or model built to test out an idea before developing it further.

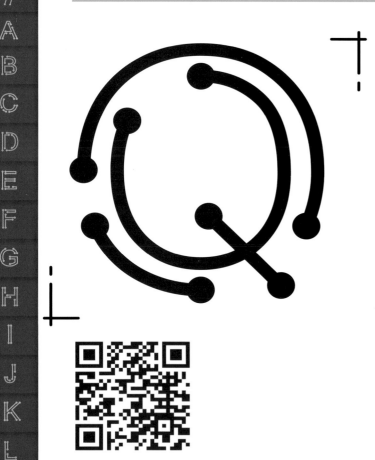

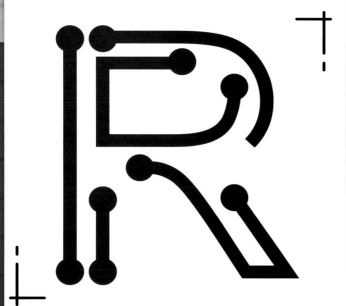

QR CODE
Noun: a square with lots of smaller square and rectangular shapes inside that can be scanned by a device and used to launch a website.

REAL-TIME TRANSLATION
Noun: software that can listen to a voice and then instantly change it into a different language. This technology is especially helpful when talking to people in other countries.

REMOTE ACCESS
Noun: a way of using or logging into a computer from somewhere far away from it.

RESOLUTION
(REZ-UH-LOO-SHUN)
Noun: the amount of detail displayed on a screen. The higher the resolution, the more detailed an image appears.

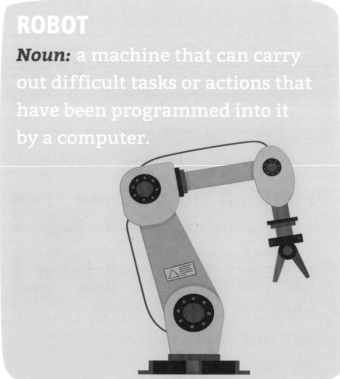

ROBOT
Noun: a machine that can carry out difficult tasks or actions that have been programmed into it by a computer.

ABCDEFGHIJKLMNOPQRSTUVWXYZ

ROBOTIC VACUUM CLEANER

Noun: a small machine that automatically cleans your floors. It's like having a personal assistant that will clean your room for you!

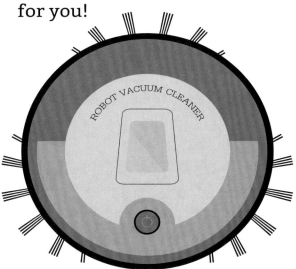

ROUTER
(ROU-TUHR)

Noun: a piece of hardware that directs wireless signals, such as an internet connection, to other electronic devices. Try turning this off and on again if your internet signal has stopped. See **HARDWARE** and **WIFI**.

WORD SEARCH

U	C	L	O	U	P	T	Y
S	Y	U	D	I	G	I	S
P	J	P	I	M	U	M	N
I	D	I	G	A	L	S	B
X	U	P	I	X	E	L	S
U	S	T	T	D	P	A	C
L	B	R	A	P	I	X	E
S	K	C	L	O	U	D	W

Can you spot some of the words from this book in these letters? Do this word search and see if you can find every one!

- CLOUD
- DIGITAL
- PIN
- PIXELS
- USB

SATELLITE

Noun: a machine that is sent into space and moves around the Earth, moon, sun, or a planet. We can use satellites to send data and signals around the world.

SATNAV

Noun: short for satellite navigation, this is a device or a piece of software that finds your location and then gives you directions to get to another place. See **SOFTWARE**.

SCANNER

Noun: hardware that allows you to transfer paper documents onto your computer as digital files. Many printers come with a built-in scanner. See **HARDWARE**.

SCREEN MIRRORING

Verb: sending the images on a computer, tablet, or smartphone screen to a TV, usually using your home Wi-Fi network. See **WI-FI**.

SCREENSHOT

Noun: an image taken of whatever is directly on a device's screen.

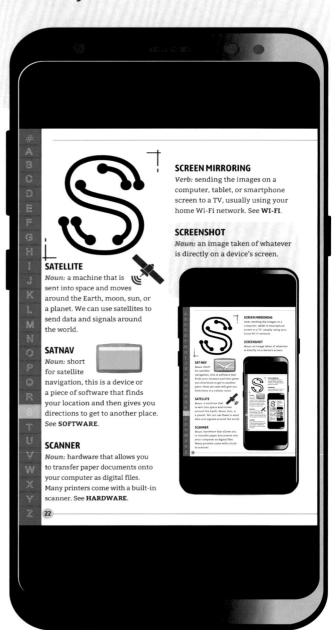

SELFIE LENS

Noun: the camera on the front of a handheld device, made to take those awesome selfies.

SELFIE STICK

Noun: a long device that you can attach to your smartphone and use for taking a selfie from farther away. This helps you to fit more people or things into the picture.

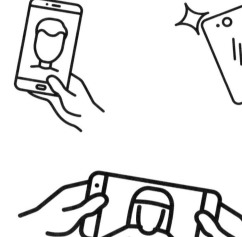

SETTINGS

Noun: an application or menu that lets you customize the way a device looks or behaves.

SMARTPHONE

Noun: a type of mobile phone that can also perform some of the functions of a computer, such as accessing the internet, editing files, and playing games.

SIM CARD

Noun: a small, flat, rectangular memory card that fits inside your phone and tells it basic information, such as your phone number, as well as helping it connect to networks.

SMART WATCH

Noun: a digital device worn on the wrist, designed to be an upgrade over an ordinary watch by including apps, a touchscreen, and a Wi-Fi connection. See **WI-FI**.

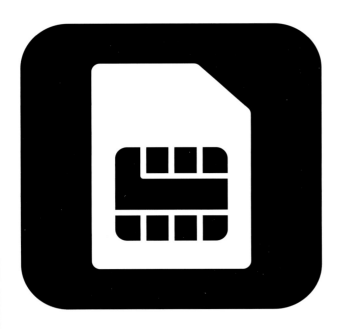

SMART HOME

Noun: a home that has been equipped with lights, heating, and other devices that can be controlled by a smartphone or virtual assistant. See **VIRTUAL ASSISTANT**.

SOFTWARE

Noun: programs that run on devices and control how pieces of technology work.

SOLAR-POWERED TECHNOLOGY

Noun: devices that use the sun's light to power or charge themselves.

DID YOU KNOW?

Some people have used this solar-powered technology to try to make solar-powered cars! They might look a bit odd – and you need to make sure you're home before sunset – but these cars are a step towards using new types of energy that won't run out.

STREAMING

Verb: watching a video file or listening to a music file at almost the same time that it is being downloaded by your computer. This way, you don't have to wait for it to be downloaded first.

SURROUND SOUND

Noun: a system involving at least three speakers, which creates the feeling of sound happening around you rather than coming from one direction.

STYLUS

Noun: a small tool that is used to write or touch buttons on a smart device.

WORD JUMBLE

Each group of letters below is a jumbled up word from this book. Can you rearrange the letters and figure out what each word is? If you're finding it a bit tricky, look through the book to check out some of the words that might be jumbled.

1. DEIWTG
2. OTBRO
3. EOHTOLBTU
4. TNSGETSI

5. BTYAETR
6. NEROD
7. AELIXGMEP
8. OKBOE

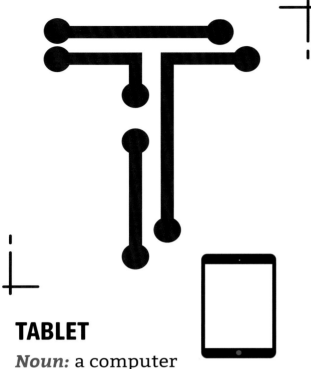

TURNTABLE

Noun: a turning, circular plate that is used by DJs to play, control, or mix a song.

TABLET

Noun: a computer without a keyboard that can be used by touching the screen with your fingers or a stylus. See **STYLUS**.

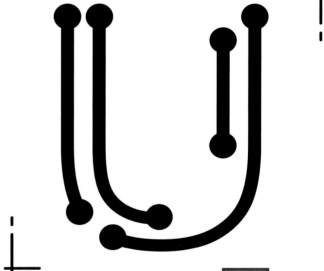

TETHERING
(TEH-THER-ING)

Noun: the linking of one device to another in order to share an internet connection.

TOUCHSCREEN

Adjective: used to describe a type of screen that can be controlled by pressing it with your fingers.

USB (Universal Serial Bus)

Initialism: a system for connecting a device to a computer.

USER INTERFACE

Noun: the way a user can interact with a computer and the options they are given to do so.

ANSWERS: 1. WIDGET 2. ROBOT 3. BLUETOOTH 4. SETTINGS 5. BATTERY 6. DRONE 7. MEGAPIXEL 8. EBOOK

ABCDEFGHIJKLMNOPQRSTUVWXYZ

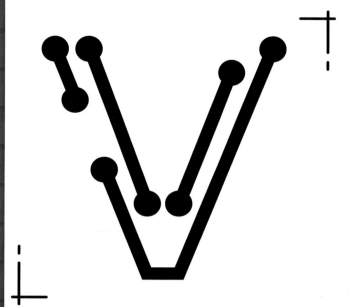

VIRTUAL ASSISTANT

Noun: software that understands voice commands and completes different tasks for the user. These are usually housed in the form of a wireless speaker. See **SOFTWARE** and **WIRELESS SPEAKER**.

VERSION

Noun: a form of a product that is different from other forms of the same product.

VIDEO CALL

Noun: a type of call that allows you to see the other person or people through their camera.

VIDEO GAME

Noun: an electronic game in which players control the characters or stories shown on a TV or computer screen.

VOICE-CONTROLLED

Adjective: the ability to be operated just by using your voice.

VR (Virtual Reality)

Initialism: a simulation of being inside a virtual, or computer-generated, world. By using a VR headset, the user can look around a virtual world and experience it as if they are inside it.

WATER-RESISTANT

Adjective: able to resist damage from water up to a certain depth and length of time. This is different from waterproof, which means water cannot damage something at all.

WEARABLE TECH

Noun: devices that are built into clothes or are designed to be worn by the user.

DID YOU KNOW?

In some countries you can buy clothes, such as jackets and coats, with air conditioning fans built into them. Yes, it is probably easier to stay cool by just not wearing the coat!

WEBCAM

Noun: a small camera that is built or plugged into your computer so that you can see and talk to people over the internet. You should only use a webcam to talk to people you know. See **VIDEO CALL**.

WEBCAST

Noun: a live event that is broadcast to lots of viewers from a website.

WIDGET
(WIH-JIHT)

Noun: a fancy shortcut that lets you use certain features of an app without completely opening the app. See **APP**.

WI-FI
(WHY-FY)
Noun: a facility that lets computers, smartphones, or other devices connect to the internet.

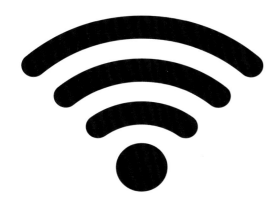

WIRELESS CHARGING
Noun: a way of supplying electric energy to battery-powered mobile devices without using any wires.

WIRELESS DEVICE
Noun: a device that sends and receives data from other places without using any wires. A common example of a wireless device is a mobile phone.

WIRELESS SPEAKER
Noun: a device that can play music over Wi-Fi or Bluetooth from a paired device such as a smartphone, tablet, computer, or TV. See **BLUETOOTH**, **PAIRING** and **WI-FI**.

WORLD WIDE WEB
Noun: a collection of web pages found on the internet.

CROSSWORD

There are many definitions in this book. How well do you know them? On a piece of paper, use the definitions below to figure out which words fit into the boxes on the grid. If you're struggling, flip through this book and try to match the definitions with the right words.

ACROSS:

3. a piece of hardware that directs wireless signals, such as an internet connection, to other electronic devices
9. programs that run on devices and control how pieces of technology work
10. the part of an electronic device that shows images to the user
11. a fancy shortcut that lets you use certain features of an app without completely opening the app
12. an error in a piece of software that stops it from working the way that it should
13. a small tool that is used to write or touch buttons on a smart device
15. a form of a product that is different from other forms of the same product
16. a type of light that we can't see, which we use in remote controls to control electronics

DOWN:

1. an area in which you can connect to a wireless internet connection
2. combinations of text, graphics, video, animation, and/or sound
4. the best or most important thing a company has produced.
5. a live event that is broadcast to lots of viewers from a website
6. a flying machine controlled remotely by someone on the ground.
7. an image that is used behind icons and widgets on your device's home screen
8. connecting two devices together, usually to transfer information
14. a device on which you can store and read an eBook

ABCDEFGHIJKLMNOPQRSTUVWXYZ